DIGITAL KIT SOFTWARE END USER LICENSE AGREEMENT

THANK YOU FOR LICENSING THE USE OF THE ACCOMPANYING SOFTWARE PRODUCT. IT IS IMPORTANT THAT YOU READ THESE TERMS CAREFULLY. THESE ARE THE ONLY TERMS AND CONDITIONS APPLICABLE TO YOUR USE OF THE SOFTWARE PRODUCT. THE SOFTWARE PRODUCT IS PROTECTED BY COPYRIGHT LAWS AND INTERNATIONAL COPYRIGHT TREATIES, AS WELL AS OTHER INTELLECTUAL PROPERTY LAWS. ALL RIGHTS NOT EXPRESSLY GRANTED TO YOU IN THIS LICENSE AGREEMENT ARE RESERVED TO DAISYTRAIL OR ITS LICENSORS. THE SOFTWARE PRODUCT IS LICENSED, NOT SOLD.

This Digital Kit Software End User License Agreement ("Agreement") is a legal agreement between you and DaisyTrail for the accompanying Software Product may include but is not limited to computer software, associated media, printed materials, and "online" or electronic documentation (all referred to as the "Software Product"). "DaisyTrail" is a trading name of Serif (Europe) Ltd which is the legal entity with which you are entering into this Agreement.

By installing, displaying, copying, accessing or otherwise using the Software Product, you are agreeing to be bound by the terms of this Agreement.

1. GRANT OF LICENSE

Subject to you complying with these terms and in consideration of your obligations and undertakings in this Agreement DaisyTrail hereby grants you a personal, non-exclusive, non-transferable license to use the Software Product according to these terms.

2. SCOPE OF USE

2.1 You may install, display, access and use the Software Product on one non-portable computer and one portable computer. The Software Product may not be used by anyone other than yourself or members of your immediate household. All such household members to be notified by you as to the terms and condition of this Agreement and shall be bound by it before they can have use of the Software Product.

2.2 "Supplied Content" shall mean any graphical or audio elements including Clipart, Fonts , Typefaces, Letter Designs, Embellishments, Backgrounds, Frames, Materials, Templates, Layouts, Quickpages, Photo Images, Video footage or Audio files supplied as part of the Software Product. "Derived Content" shall mean any work in any media which used Supplied Content in any manner as any part of its creation. "Digital Content" shall mean all Supplied Content and any Derived Content.

2.3 Your rights to use Digital Content are limited to for Personal Use only and any Commercial Use is strictly prohibited. If you are uncertain as to whether any intended use complies with these terms you should seek the advice of an attorney or legal counsel. If you wish to use Digital Content for Commercial Use please contact DaisyTrail for details of our commercial licenses.

2.4 "Personal Use" means use for your normal or customary personal purposes. Your rights to distribute Digital Content are limited to use as part of printed personal use documents and electronic distribution as part of a personal use document where:

(a) the Digital Content embedded within that personal use document is within a static graphic image such as a "jpg" or within an embedded electronic document and;

(b) the distributed Digital Content is in a secure format that permits only the viewing and printing and not the editing, altering, enhancing or modifying of such static graphic or embedded electronic document.

2.5 "Commercial Use" shall include but not be limited to:

(a) any tangible item distributed for a fee;

(b) any business flyer, form or sign;

(c) any use that would be perceived as for Commercial Use in any capacity.

2.6 You may not use Digital Content:

(a) to create scandalous, obscene, defamatory, or immoral works using the Digital Content nor use the Digital Content for any purpose prohibited by law;

(b) except as expressly permitted by this Agreement;

3. PROHIBITIONS

3.1 Except as permitted elsewhere in this Agreement you shall not:-

(a) alter the Software Product for the purpose of adding any functionality which such Software Product did not have when supplied to you by DaisyTrail.

(b) assign, rent, transfer, distribute, sell, disclose, deal in, make available or grant any rights in the Software Product or any copy thereof in any form to any person.

(c) remove alter, obscure, interfere with or add to any proprietary notices, labels, trade marks, names or marks on, annexed to, or contained within the Software Product;

(d) use the Software Product in any manner that infringes the intellectual property or other rights of DaisyTrail or any other party.

3.2. For any use of Software Product other than as expressly permitted by this Agreement and without prejudice to any other right or remedy you hereby indemnify and shall keep indemnified DaisyTrail, its licensors and authorised distributors against all and any claims actions, liability, costs, proceedings, awards, damages, losses, demands, expenses, fines, loss of profits, penalties, loss of reputation, judgements and any other liabilities including legal costs (without set-off counterclaim or reduction) suffered by DaisyTrail and/or its licensors and /or its authorised distributors arising out of or in connection with the use of the Software Product by you and/or any of your clients whether or not such losses were foreseeable or foreseen at the date of this Agreement.

4. INTELLECTUAL PROPERTY RIGHTS AND TERMINATION

You acknowledge that:

4.1 all title to the copyright and all other intellectual property rights in and to the Software Product, its accompanying documentation and any copy made by You are the exclusive property of and remain with DaisyTrail and/or its licensor(s),

4.2 the Software Product and all copies thereof are DaisyTrail's exclusive property and constitute confidential information and a valuable trade secret of DaisyTrail.

5. LIMITED WARRANTY AND DISCLAIMER

DaisyTrail warrants that for a period of thirty (30) days after delivery to you that any CD-ROMs or DVD-ROMs on which the Software Product is supplied will, under normal use, be free from defects that prevent you from loading the Software Product on to a computer. DaisyTrail's entire liability and your exclusive remedy under this warranty will be, at DaisyTrail's option, to (a) use reasonable commercial efforts to attempt to correct or work around errors, or (b) to replace the Software Product with a functionally equivalent Software Product, on a CD-ROM or DVD-ROM, or as applicable or (c) return the price paid for the Software Product, in each case subject to you having paid for the Software Product in full and upon return of the Software Product to DaisyTrail together with a copy of your receipt for its purchase. This Limited Warranty shall not apply if failure of the Software Product media has resulted from accident, abuse, misuse or misapplication. Any replacement Software Product will be warranted for the remainder of the original warranty period or thirty (30) days from delivery to you, whichever is longer. Outside the United Kingdom, neither these remedies nor any product support services offered by DaisyTrail are available without proof of purchase from a distributor authorized by DaisyTrail. The Software Product is licensed on an "as is" basis without any warranty of any nature.

6. NO OTHER WARRANTIES

Except for the above express limited warranty, all warranties conditions, terms and duties either expressed or implied by law and relating to merchantability, quality, fitness and/or non-infringement with regard to the Software Product and the provision of or failure to provide support services are excluded to the fullest extent permitted by law. You shall be solely responsible for the selection, use, efficiency and suitability of the Software Product and DaisyTrail shall have no liability therefor. DaisyTrail shall have no liability for, nor obligation to indemnify you regarding actions alleging the infringement of proprietary rights by the Software Product. DaisyTrail does not warrant that the

operation of the Software Product will be uninterrupted or error free or that the Software Product will meet your specific requirements. Nothing in this Agreement shall exclude or limit any statutory rights which cannot be excluded or limited due to you acting as a consumer. Any provisions which would be void under any legislation shall to that extent have no force or effect

7. LIMITATION OF LIABILITY

In no event will DaisyTrail or its suppliers be liable for loss and/or corruption of data, loss of profits, damage to goodwill, cost of cover, any pure economic, special, incidental, punitive, exemplary, consequential or indirect damages or losses and/or any business interruption, loss of business, loss of contracts, loss of opportunity and/or loss of production arising from or in connection with the use of the Software Product, however caused. Each limitation will apply even if DaisyTrail or its authorized distributor has been advised of the possibility of such damage and shall be deemed to be repeated and apply as a separate provision for each of liability in contract, tort, breach of a statutory duty, breach of common law and/or under any other legal basis. In no event will DaisyTrail's liability exceed the amount you paid for the Software Product. You acknowledges that these limitations are necessary to allow DaisyTrail to provide the Software Product at its current prices. If modification to these limitations is required DaisyTrail will agree appropriate amendment for payment of a higher than current price for the Software Product. Nothing in this Agreement shall exclude or limit DaisyTrail's liability for death or personal injury due to its negligence or any liability due to its fraud or any other liability which may not be limited or excluded as a matter of law.

8. TERMINATION

You may terminate this Agreement at any time. DaisyTrail may terminate this Agreement if you fail to fully comply with the terms and conditions of this Agreement. In either event all licenses granted under this Agreement shall end immediately and you must destroy all copies of the Software Product. All terms which by their nature should survive termination of this Agreement shall survive its termination.

9. MISCELLANEOUS

9.1 This Agreement shall be governed by and interpreted in accordance with English law and not by the 1980 U. N. Convention on Contracts for the International Sale of Goods. If this Agreement has been translated into a language which is not English and a dispute arises as to the meaning/ translation of any term of this Agreement, the interpretation of the English version shall prevail. The parties agree to submit to the exclusive jurisdiction of the English Courts.

9.2 Except to the extent of any misrepresentation or breach of warranty which constitutes fraud this Agreement constitutes the entire agreement between DaisyTrail and you and supersedes all prior agreements, understandings, communications, advertising, proposals or representations, oral or written, by either party.

9.3 If any provision of this Agreement is held invalid, illegal or unenforceable by a court of competent jurisdiction, such provision shall be severed and if possible revised to the extent necessary to cure the invalidity, illegality or non-enforceability, and the remainder of this Agreement shall continue in full force and effect.

9.4 Any change to this Agreement shall only be valid if it is in writing and signed by an authorized representative of both DaisyTrail and you.

9.5 No failure, delay, relaxation or forbearance on the part of either party in exercising any power or right under this Agreement shall operate as a waiver of such power or right or of any other power or right.

9.6 This Agreement and the license granted pursuant to this Agreement are personal to you and except where permitted above you shall not assign the benefit of or any interest or obligation under this Agreement.

9.7 Apart from DaisyTrail's licensors and authorised distributors, a person who is not a party to this Agreement has no right under the Contracts (Rights of Third Parties) Act 1999 or otherwise to enforce any term of this Agreement. The consent of any third party is not required for any variation (including any release or compromise of any liability under this Agreement) or termination of this Agreement.

At the Zoo

At the

Zoo

123!8&

abcABC

Brushes

Frames

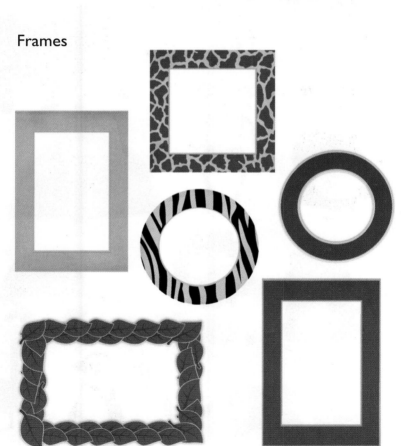

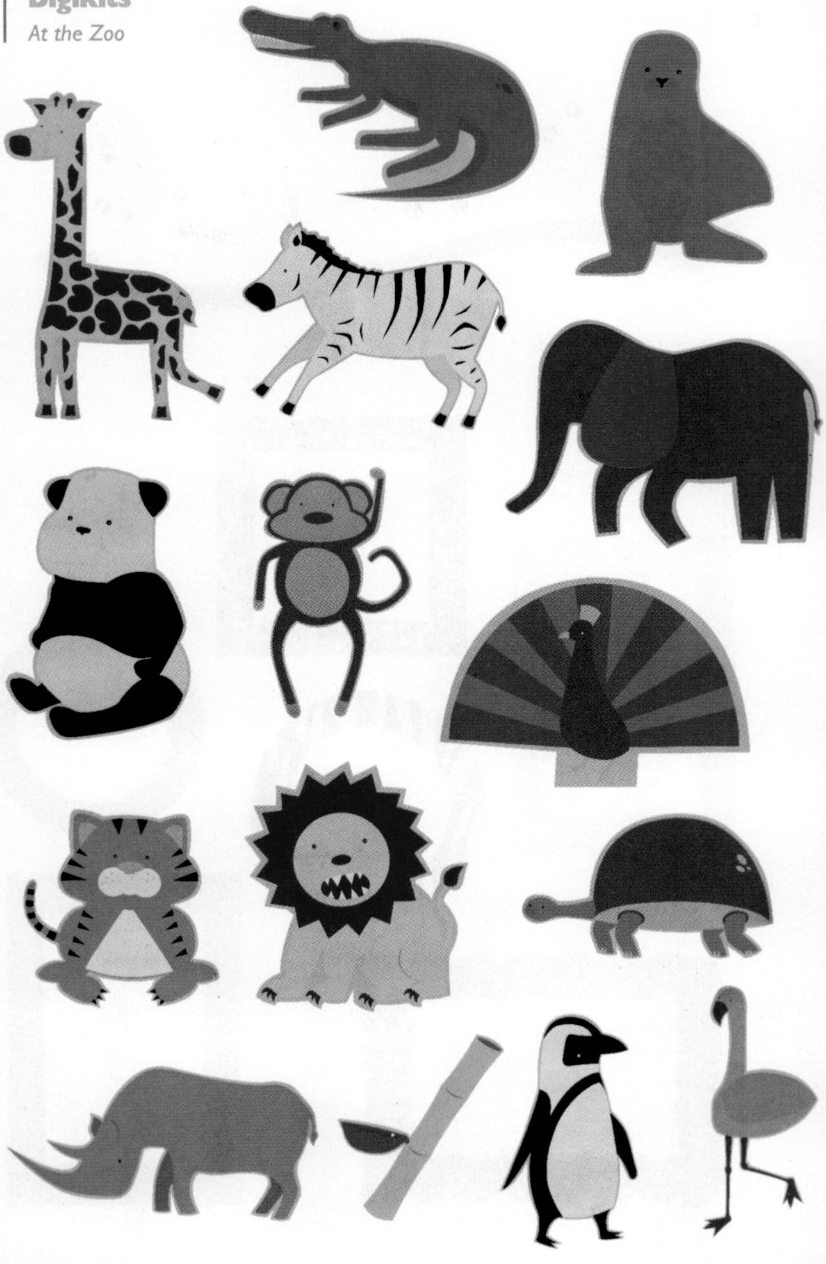

Sample Layouts

Plus **6 extra layouts** included on the DVD!

Materials

Backgrounds

Cake Shop

Cake

Shop

123!:&

abcABC

Brushes

Frames

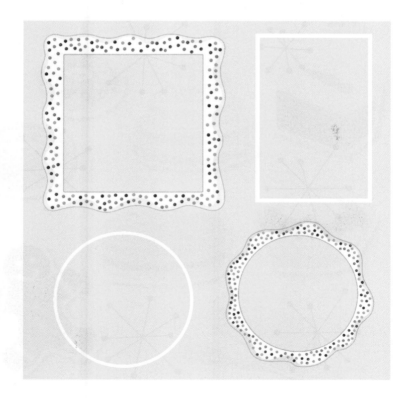

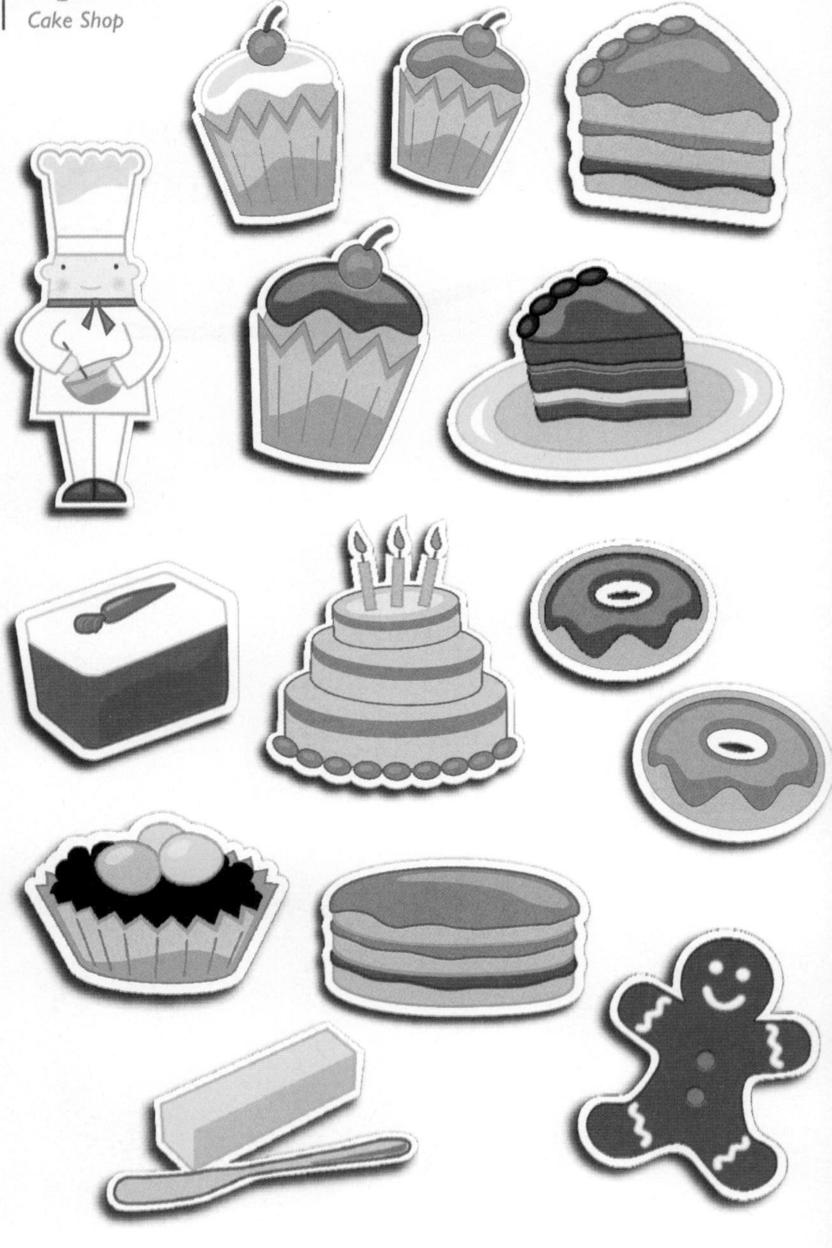

Plus **8 extra layouts** included on the DVD!

Materials

Backgrounds

Dinosaurs

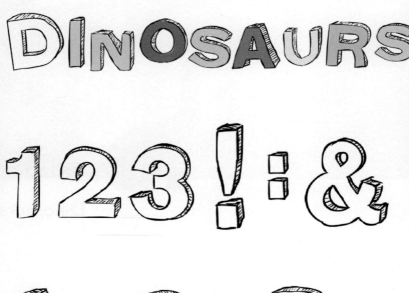

Brushes

Frames

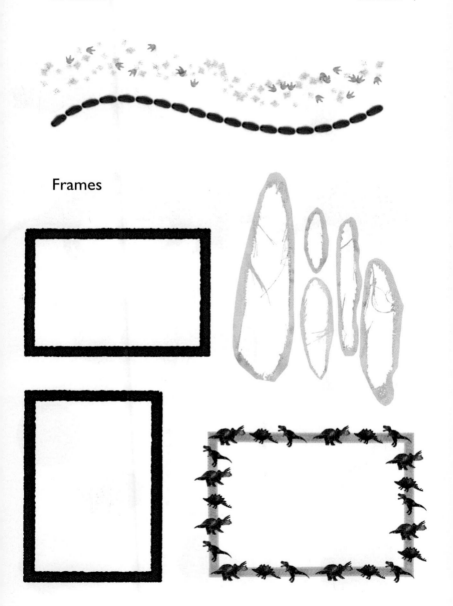

Embellishments

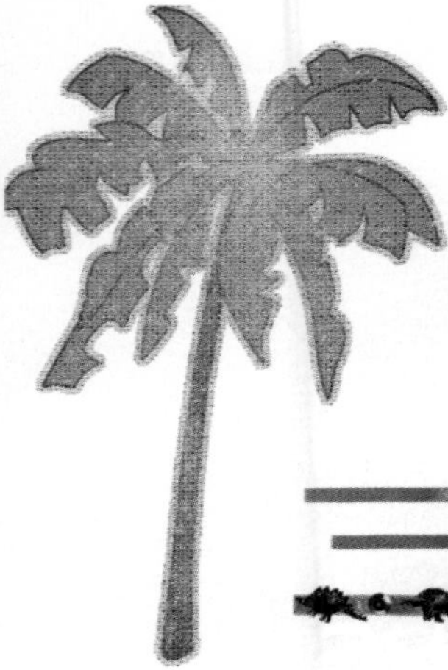

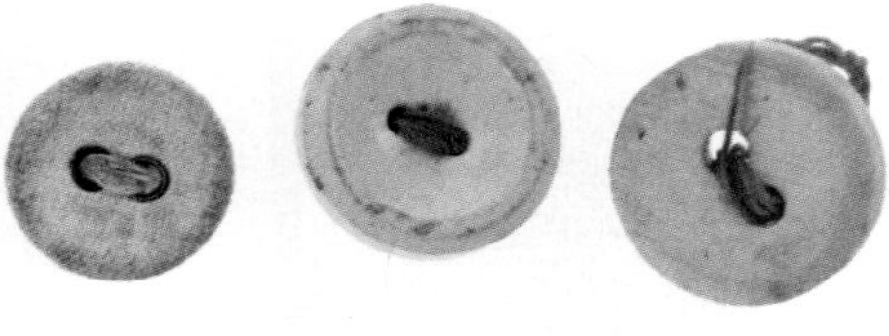

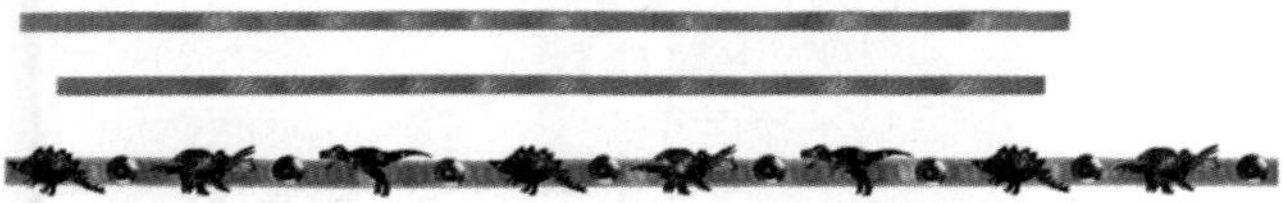

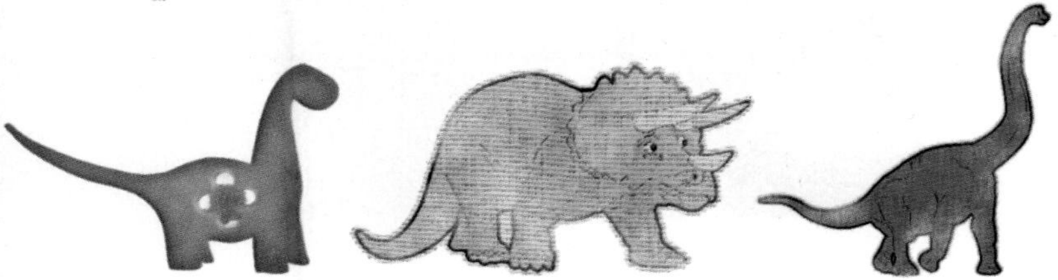

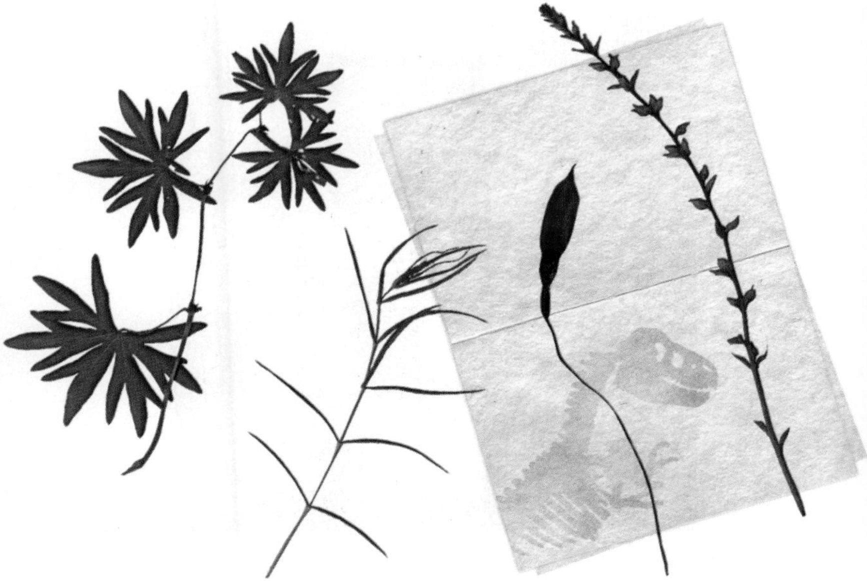

Sample Layouts

Materials

Backgrounds

Past Present Future Family

Family Tree

Family

Tree

123!:&

abc ABC

Brushes

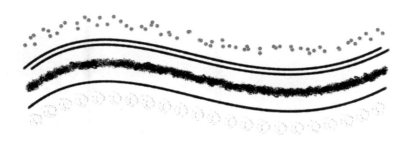

Frames

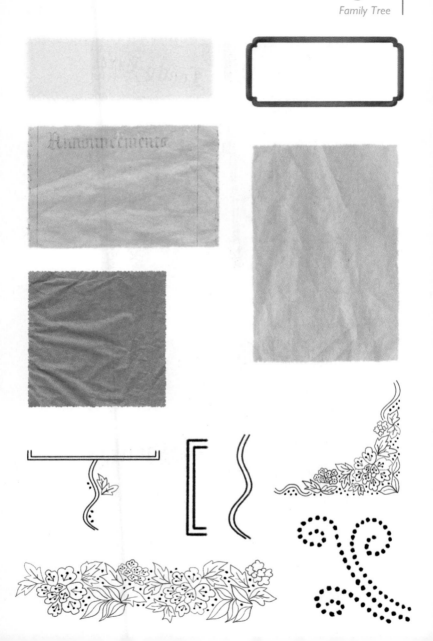

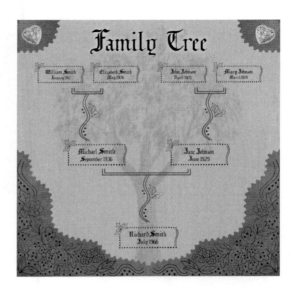

Materials

Backgrounds

Ladies Night

Ladies

Night

123 !:&

abc ABC

Brushes

Frames

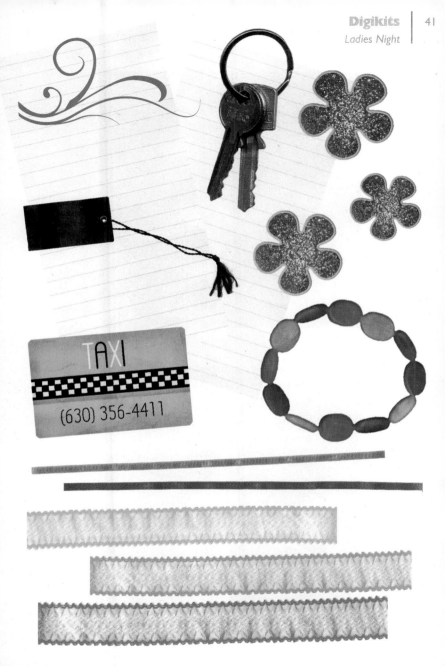

Sample Layouts

Plus **2 extra layouts** included on the DVD!

Materials

Backgrounds

Paper Forest

Brushes

Frames

Embellishments

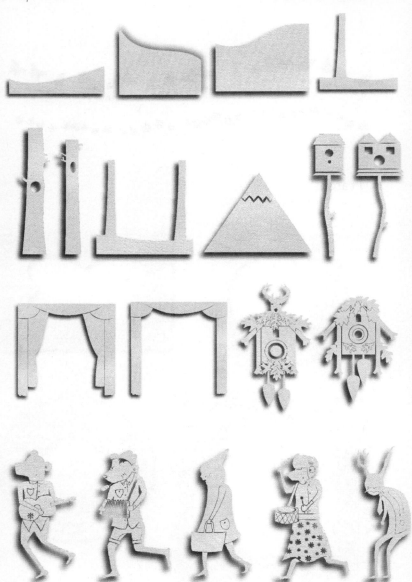

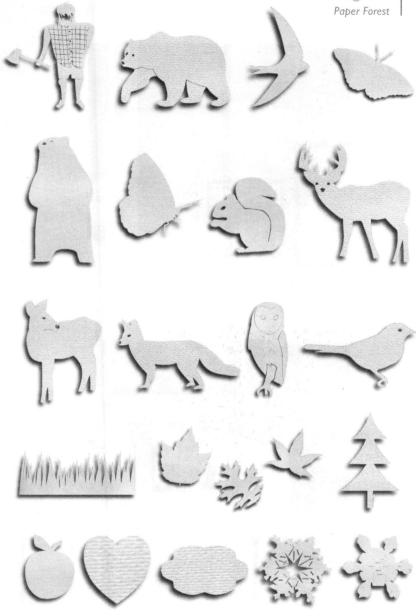

Materials

Backgrounds

Pirates

Pirates

123 !:&

abc ABC

Brushes

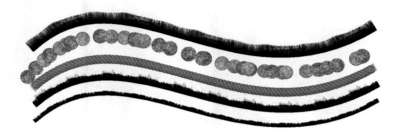

Frames

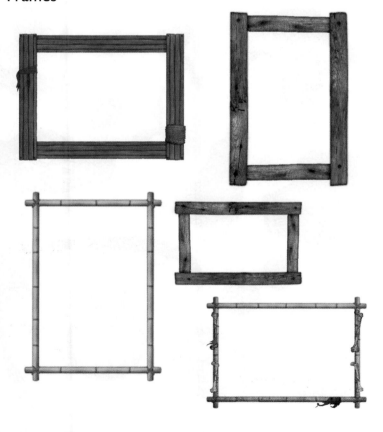

Plus **4 extra layouts** included on the DVD!

Materials

Backgrounds

Rambling

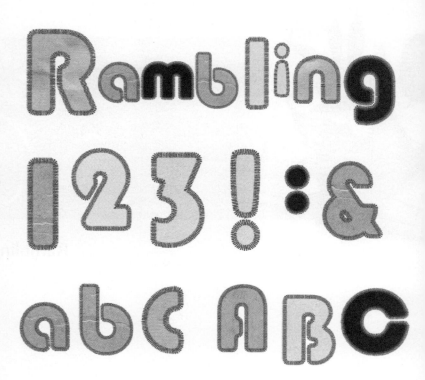

Brushes

Frames

Embellishments

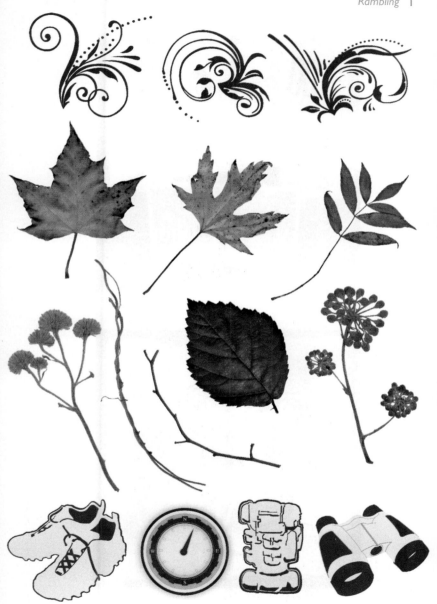

Sample Layouts

Materials

Backgrounds

Sketch Spirits

Sketch

Spirits

123 ! : &

abc ABC

Brushes

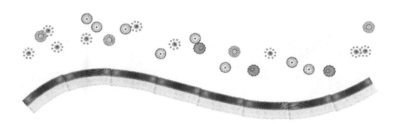

Frames

Embellishments

Plus **2 extra layouts** included on the DVD!

Materials

Backgrounds

Vintage Sideshow

Brushes

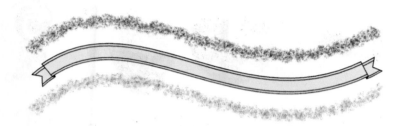

Frames

Embellishments

Sample Layouts

Plus **2 extra layouts** included on the DVD!

Materials

Backgrounds